Oscar Enrique Correa Miranda
Nieves Maria Melo Miranda

# Management Systems

Oscar Enrique Correa Miranda
Nieves Maria Melo Miranda

# Management Systems

## Free Software

ScienciaScripts

**Imprint**

Any brand names and product names mentioned in this book are subject to trademark, brand or patent protection and are trademarks or registered trademarks of their respective holders. The use of brand names, product names, common names, trade names, product descriptions etc. even without a particular marking in this work is in no way to be construed to mean that such names may be regarded as unrestricted in respect of trademark and brand protection legislation and could thus be used by anyone.

Cover image: www.ingimage.com

This book is a translation from the original published under ISBN 978-613-9-43344-5.

Publisher:
Sciencia Scripts
is a trademark of
Dodo Books Indian Ocean Ltd. and OmniScriptum S.R.L publishing group

120 High Road, East Finchley, London, N2 9ED, United Kingdom
Str. Armeneasca 28/1, office 1, Chisinau MD-2012, Republic of Moldova, Europe
Printed at: see last page
**ISBN: 978-620-8-20744-1**

# SUMMARY

# CHAPTER I

## NIEVES MARÍA MELO MIRANDA

Nowadays it is necessary to understand that the management world is a truly fascinating place, where decisions can be taken that directly influence organisations.In this sense, reference is nowadays made to smart indicators, which allow managers to make coherent decisions that can be measured and that positively impact on the performance of the organisation. In this sense, it is necessary to understand that today's companies need to achieve concrete results, as they are immersed in changing markets where technology and innovation set the standard for business productivity.

**Sistema de Recursos Humanos**

Nombre     Posición     Agregar Empleado

enrique - escritor

Source: https://infune.blogspot.com/ Human resources system.

When dealing with management systems, it is necessary to understand that human resources play a fundamental role in the development of companies and organisations, which is why it is essential to integrate a human resources system that takes into consideration the name of the person and the position they hold within the organisation. This human resource system will be able to store the name and position, so that when it is necessary to be able to have available in time this human resource so indispensable nowadays that when you want to solve a problem or generate a project it becomes intellectual capital. The new system is in full action that triggers a lot of positive things to boost the organisation's productivity.

**Sistema de Mercadeo**



Source: https://infune.blogspot.com/ Marketing system.

It is also necessary to understand that in any company or institution, the importance of showing or making known to others the product or service that is being elaborated must be clear. In this sense, in this research a system is developed to attend the marketing department in which reference is made to the advertising campaign and the type of activity that is being carried out, so that from a managerial level, the impact that it can have on the level of productivity in the institution can be followed up.

**Sistema de Mercadeo**



Source: https://infune.blogspot.com/ Marketing System.

It is necessary to understand that many campaigns may be focused within the framework of a social network, but if you try to develop a management system that incorporates computer and mathematical tools to support business leadership, from a local server this can have a major impact on global search engines.If this hypothesis were to be fulfilled in six months, this would allow the company to achieve its mission from a double perspective. On the one hand, it would be fulfilling the possibility of incorporating management tools into the global management system, and on the other hand, the level of acceptance based on technological innovation with an educational and functional character could have an important impact on global search engines, which in turn would allow the organic growth of the network or management system.



Source: https://infune.blogspot.com/ Efficiency system departments.

In this example, a programme integrated to the management system is developed, which allows to study the level of efficiency in three departments focused on sales, production and marketing. It is necessary to understand that when a management system is being developed and there is a motivation because the knowledge is based on high-level programming languages, this can have a direct impact on a high level of efficiency in terms of software production by the production department.

Source: https://infune.blogspot.com/ Efficiency system departments.

It is necessary to point out that the incorporation of this type of calculator in a management system is fundamental, as it will make it possible to quantify the level of objectives set and how many have been fully achieved so far.In the practical example given above, 50% efficiency is revealed, obviously when 50% of the objectives have been met, efficiency will also be in the order of 50%, which is totally logical and reasonable, but when incorporating this system in the production processes, it is possible to take into account those intelligent objectives that must be measurable and achievable over a certain period of time.

## Matriz de Eficacia de Departamentos



Source: https://infune.blogspot.com/ Departmental effectiveness matrix.

In this case, a system based on a matrix is proposed that evaluates the sales, marketing and production departments taking into consideration the level of efficiency, in this table the level of objectives achieved by each department can be seen and which objectives have been established.Having a management system that takes into consideration the human resources, marketing, production and sales departments definitely represents the possibility of integrating those processes in which activities are developed that may be qualitatively good but that quantitatively deserve exhaustive monitoring on a weekly basis.

**Matriz de Eficacia de Departamentos**

| Departamento | Objetivos Alcanzados | Objetivos Establecidos |
|---|---|---|
| Ventas | 2 | 5 |
| Marketing | 2 | 5 |
| Producción | 2 | 5 |

Calcular Eficacia

**Eficacia Total: 40.00%**

Source: https://infune.blogspot.com/ Matríz eficacia.

In this case, when running the matrix calculator, three departments are taken into consideration, and the possibility of a compliance focused on two objectives achieved out of a total of five results in an effectiveness level of 40%. In this case the three departments addressed for the object of study were marketing, sales and production, understanding that at present companies and organisations are in the so-called knowledge society, in which interactions occur between people in a matter of seconds and reliability in a company can be won or lost instantly, having 40% effectiveness in these three departments would obviously be necessary to maintain the credibility of the operations carried out in the company based on honesty, values and altruism.

In order to try to promote an action plan that takes into consideration new ideas and technologies based on artificial intelligence, in the production department being the case of a management system, new graphics must be progressively incorporated that lead to a better analysis of the reality that is being generated in each of the departments within the company.

At first, these graphs and statistics may not be of interest to all the public that accesses the management system, however, when trying to promote a presentation to explain the benefits of integrating equations of imaginary irrational numbers and matrices in a management system, these graphs can be of fundamental importance for other companies to understand the efforts that are being made from the integration of the management system. of a management system that allows for expansion by taking into consideration the progressive use of mathematics and its formulas.



Source: https://infune.blogspot.com/ Relationship departments.

Nowadays, when referring to intelligent indicators, these must be possible, that is why in this research a management system is developed, which is mounted on a local Host server that interacts with SQL database, programs are executed taking into consideration PHP Java Script CSS and HTML. This system integration allows the measurement of internal departments in terms of their efficiency taking into consideration calculations made from the mathematical perspective focused on imaginary numbers, irrational and matrices based on the measurement of the various processes in the departments of a company that is dedicated to producing social networks.



Source: https://infune.blogspot.com/ Complex equations calculator.

In this case, a model was developed based on the calculation of complex equations, in which we try to compare, for example, the performance between two departments of the social media company.

This type of system allows managers to mathematically manage the actual performance of two departments, in the case of a social network, obviously it must have one department in charge of marketing and another in charge of content production.

To create an equation with imaginary numbers and solve it in the context of a management system, we can consider a practical example. Suppose we are analysing the performance of two departments in a company, where each department has a performance represented by a complex number.

In a managerial system, this equation could be interpreted as the combination of the performances of two departments, where the real part (x) represents tangible performance (e.g. revenue) and the imaginary part (y) could represent intangible factors (e.g. customer satisfaction).

Source: https://infune.blogspot.com/ addition, subtraction, division and multiplication.

It is necessary to understand that nowadays when referring to a company that generates a social network, within the framework of the intelligent objectives, a monthly growth goal must be established, based on new users for the network. That is why it is necessary to generate innovative content from the content creation department, but definitely the manager of the marketing department has to know how to link all the content that is being created to the social network. The new ideas are generated so that new creative ideas can be brought to the market and this raises compliance with the user growth table set up in the network.

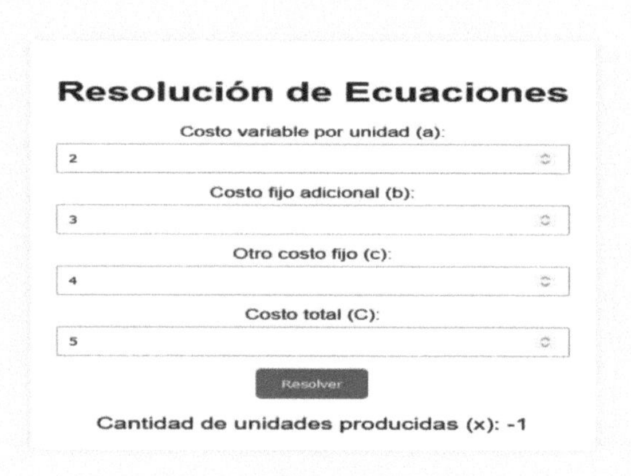



Source: https://infune.blogspot.com/ Units produced.

Nowadays, it is necessary for any management system to be able to take into consideration the units produced during each month. That is why in this research a series of calculators were developed from programming code, which allows to manage and evaluate the cost in each department of the company, in order to be able to take into consideration the units that have been produced. The object of study establishes a management system, which incorporates the development and implementation of a server, applications and calculators that will definitely allow the establishment of a mathematical model that manages to quantify the processes and relationships that occur in the departments within the organisation through imaginary and irrational numbers and matrices.

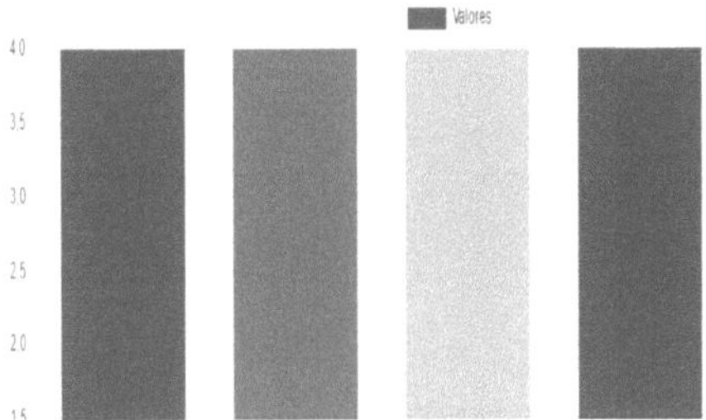


Source: https://infune.blogspot.com/ Values of units produced.

It is necessary to understand that this final result can be evaluated on a monthly basis from each department, in the case under study a social network definitely needs to start seeing the growth of its users as soon as possible in order to be able to establish commercial relationships with other companies. In the case study, a management system is developed, which incorporates server technology, applications, databases together with programmes and calculators, in order to give theoretical and practical support to the activities that are developed within the institution. In the case of a university, there is obviously a department for the control of studies, human resources, management and others. In function of these, a record of the teaching and administrative staff can be kept in a component of the system, which in this case would be the human resources system.

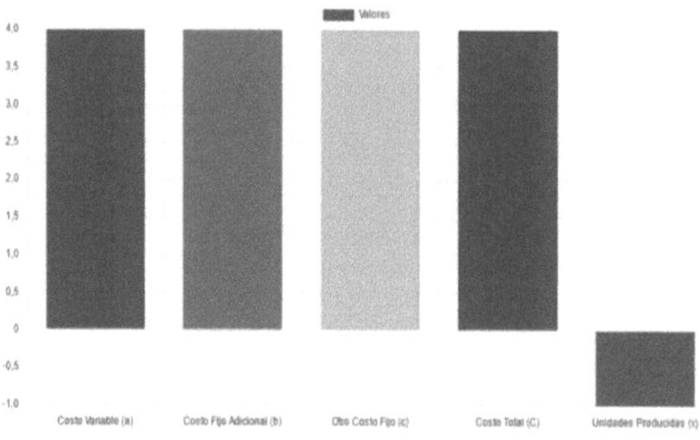


Source: https://infune.blogspot.com/ Component values.

In this case, the aim is to promote a social network with the integration of various departments, which allows the integration of followers worldwide while maintaining a scheme of truly achievable objectives. It is necessary to take into account some successful companies in the market, at some point in the development of production processes can be an important reference to take into consideration.In the investigation it was possible to develop a mathematical model, which allows to calculate the effectiveness, efficiency, relations of the departments, the intention is to incorporate technologies that allow in the long term to reduce the costs and to be much more productive. It is necessary to understand that the use of artificial intelligence, comes to be an important element to dynamise the graphic processes or the simulation of events, which allows at the research level to understand the importance of incorporating a new technology and its possible application.

Source: https://infune.blogspot.com/ Equation solving.

In that case it is necessary to highlight that there have been social networking companies that have managed to reach more than one billion downloads of their applications, in that sense it is necessary to emphasise that starting from a traditional server scheme is something important but thinking in terms of the short term, at the latest one year, in the possibility of projecting the social network towards global schemes, then definitely integrating the application scheme in the processes for downloading globally in terms of Android and iOS systems must be an achievable priority in the short term for every manager of management systems. Establishing a mathematical model that allows for the calculation of complex, irrational equations and matrices in the organisation will allow for an in-depth understanding of those situations that are developing within the organisation at a qualitative level, but which, when evaluated at a quantitative level, can begin to monitor their evolution. Obviously, this technology must be accompanied by other types of systems, which can be linked to the performance of each department, in this sense, human resources, marketing and production can have their own systems according to their needs.

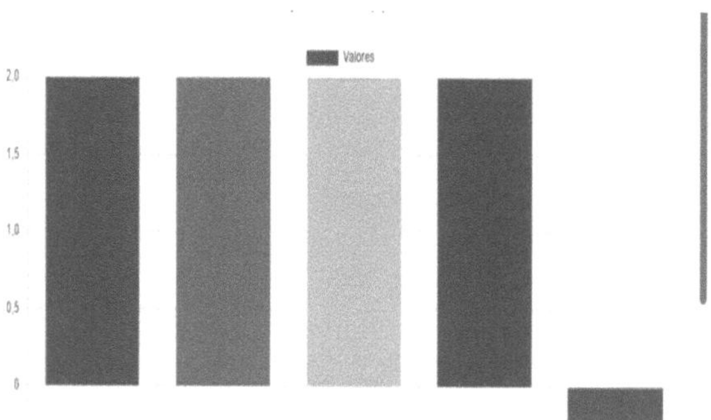


Source: https://infune.blogspot.com/ Units produced.

Definitely when a lecture focused on management systems is given at university, the participants arrive with high expectations, especially those who are in the process of training as marketing, administrative or business managers. In this sense, it is necessary to give the wings that they want to all those students who are eager for knowledge, and the first priority in the class should be to try to discover what their motivations are. When a Localhost server is set up to develop a management system, files can be added on an ongoing basis, so that the processes in the organisation can be improved on a daily basis. It is necessary to understand that this system is executed from a computer in the organisation that, when configured as a server, can support internal and external processes. In order to use these mathematical tools based on the calculations of complex numbers, irrational numbers and matrices, which can lead to evaluate the productivity of the departments, their relationships, effectiveness and efficiency, in order to advance quantitatively in the effective management of the organisation.

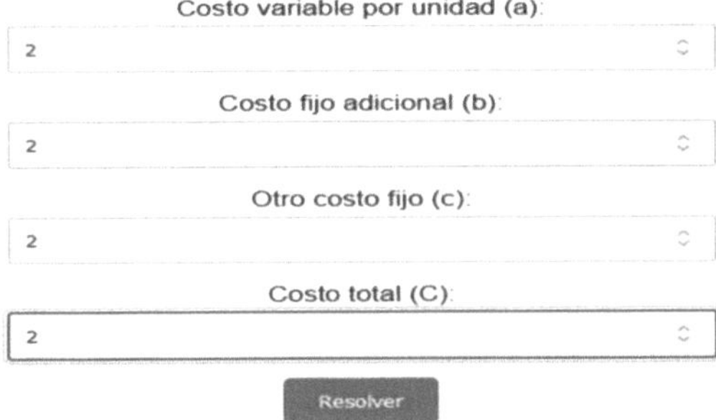



Source: https://infune.blogspot.com/ Total cost.

It is necessary to understand that also a business leader can find himself in the situation or need to implement a management system, and this can motivate workers to start meeting those goals set in the smart indicators. In the case of a company focused on the development of social networks, it is necessary to understand that it must incorporate staff focused on the area of programming and graphic design, which must work together to achieve those objectives set at the management level, and that undoubtedly should not only be focused on gaining new users but have the necessary tools available to engage those people to use the social network daily, and thus the financial business area can grow more and more every day.

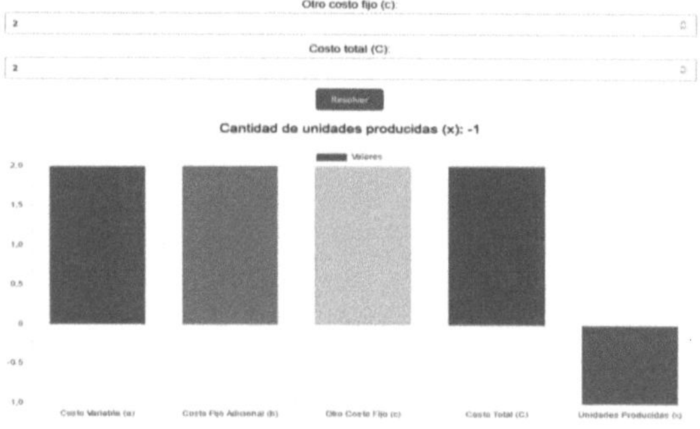

Source: https://infune.blogspot.com/ Costs and units produced.

It is definitely a fascinating challenge to develop a management system for a technology company focused on social networks, which must incorporate programming tools in order to quantify all those processes that are being developed in the company's departments.

When teaching a lecture focused on management systems development, one should definitely take into consideration the perception of the participants, as some of them may have held management positions in the area of human resources, finance or marketing.

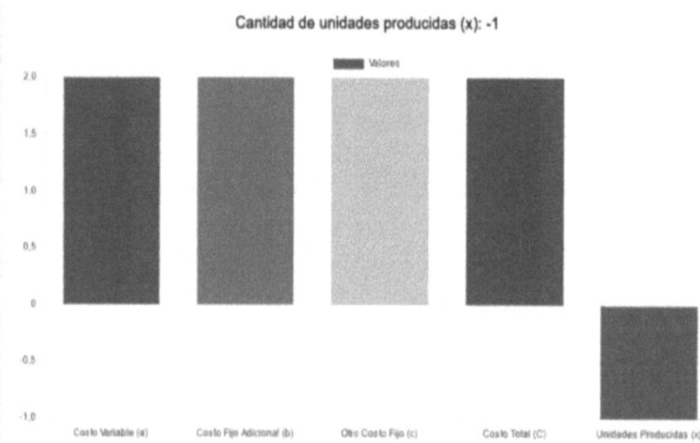

Source: https://infune.blogspot.com/ Units produced.

In this sense, it is necessary to understand that any process leader who is currently trying to implement smart metrics must understand that incorporating these types of charting systems allows all stakeholders and departments to understand the processes that are taking place. Definitely establish indicators that give relevance in the short term to the social network will be something fundamental, in that sense to establish a technological infrastructure of hardware and software that allows to develop the integration of artificial intelligence systems such as voice recognition today is a fundamental role that undoubtedly comes to represent an element of interaction of great dynamics for the social network that will be interpreted as something positive from the level of users. In the object of study, a social network is developed that incorporates SQL structured databases, in which tables such as comments, users, messages and likes will be managed.

| Nombre | Fecha de modificación | Tipo | Tamaño |
|---|---|---|---|
| comments.sql | 6/9/2024 1:54 a. m. | Archivo SQL | 1 KB |
| index | 6/9/2024 1:49 a. m. | Firefox HTML Doc... | 1 KB |
| likes.sql | 6/9/2024 1:54 a. m. | Archivo SQL | 1 KB |
| messages.sql | 6/9/2024 1:55 a. m. | Archivo SQL | 1 KB |
| posts.sql | 6/9/2024 1:53 a. m. | Archivo SQL | 1 KB |
| register | 6/9/2024 1:51 a. m. | Archivo PHP | 1 KB |
| users.sql | 6/9/2024 1:52 a. m. | Archivo SQL | 1 KB |

Source: https://infune.blogspot.com/ Databases management system.

In the object of study a system is built from a Localhost server that can store 100 GB of storage, which is an infrastructure that in the first three months of operation of the management system will allow internal and external users to perform their various activities. A SQL database is established, because the main function of the management system is to provide users with management tools, which, when implemented from a practical viewpoint using imaginary, irrational equations and matrices, allow users to develop practical calculations to track intelligent indicators within organisations and to understand what is happening within their departments in a quantifiable and logical way.

**Registro**

Nombre de usuario:

hola

Email:

s

Contraseña:

Registrarse

Source: https://infune.blogspot.com/ Email management system.

From the Back End view in the system made with the PHP programming language, CRUD tools can be incorporated, which allow to create, read and update data within the management system. The registration of secure passwords within this management system is essential, so the Password hash function is implemented, which from the Back End view of PHP gives greater security to the passwords that users store within the management system. When you develop a management system that is based on the development of applications and mathematical calculators that perform calculations with imaginary, irrational numbers and matrices, you can have tools that, by introducing data regarding a department or process, will allow you to systematically evaluate a situation, linked to the effectiveness, efficiency or relationships between processes and departments.

# Registro

Nombre de usuario:

Email:

Contraseña:

Registrarse

Source: https://infune.blogspot.com/ Password management system.

The validation of data within the system plays a fundamental role, which is why it is necessary to validate each user's login information. It is therefore important that users can enter a type of password into the system that combines capital initials, letters with numbers and symbols, thus trying to promote a much more secure use of the system. It is necessary to incorporate user and system manuals into the management system. In the first case, the focus is on everything related to the theoretical approach of people surfing the internet to the system, which in principle can be presented as a friendly social network that can be operated from the view of the object, i.e. they can simply press the buttons on the screen to start using the calculator services presented in the social network.

| Nombre | Fecha de modificación | Tipo | Tamaño |
|---|---|---|---|
| comments.sql | 6/9/2024 2:09 a. m. | Archivo SQL | 1 KB |
| index | 6/9/2024 2:11 a. m. | Firefox HTML Doc... | 1 KB |
| likes.sql | 6/9/2024 2:10 a. m. | Archivo SQL | 1 KB |
| messages.sql | 6/9/2024 2:10 a. m. | Archivo SQL | 1 KB |
| posts.sql | 6/9/2024 2:09 a. m. | Archivo SQL | 1 KB |
| register | 6/9/2024 2:12 a. m. | Archivo PHP | 1 KB |
| users.sql | 6/9/2024 2:08 a. m. | Archivo SQL | 1 KB |

Source: https://infune.blogspot.com/ Archives management system.

But it is also important to present a social network system manual with a management system approach, which is why the screenshots of each of the files and databases that make up the system are presented. From the point of view of the Back End it is necessary to understand that any management system with a social network approach can be expanded according to the technological innovations that are emerging in reality. It is important to establish a mathematical triad that provides quantitative elements for decision-making through the use of calculators, which, when integrated into the management system, will allow the leader of the processes to take the necessary actions to improve productivity. In this case, SQL databases are taken into consideration in order to keep a record of the users of the system and their online activities.



Source: https://infune.blogspot.com/ Login management system.

This is why it is necessary to show how to log in and register to the system, which from the Front End perspective is presented in a friendly way, so that users can feel completely familiar with the system they are using to motivate them to register, which would be ideal in this case to increase the level of users within the system that is intended to promote.

Source: https://infune.blogspot.com/ Management system register.

In this case the registration is represented by the name, email and password of the user, which will be stored in a SQL database, within the Localhost server. In order to guarantee the use of the system 24 hours a day, it is necessary to take into consideration the traditional electrical network, but also, the incorporation of solar panels as an alternative energy source is a truly fundamental element to give it the necessary continuity that users are expecting at a global level. It is necessary to understand that by developing a management system, taking into consideration a mathematical model, which integrates imaginary, irrational numbers and matrices, it is possible to address the relationships, effectiveness and efficiency of the departments, which make up the organisation. By clearly understanding that by adding applications that can be installed on the smart phone, it is possible to evaluate and perform calculations at any time, as it is done by decisions need to be made, and when you look at developments and graphs, you can have a better understanding of what is going on in the organisation.

**Departamentos de Redes Sociales**

**Marketing**
Responsable de la promoción y publicidad.

**Contenido**
Encargado de la creación y gestión de contenido

**Analítica**
Se enfoca en el análisis de datos y métricas.

Source: https://infune.blogspot.com/ Social media departments.

On many occasions it has been observed in some financial systems at a global level, that when the user tries to access it generates a message that the server is under maintenance, in the case of a social network that implements calculators to provide management support to companies and institutions, it is necessary to understand that it is always necessary to have a backup of the information on a server in the cloud, so that when it is necessary to restore the service it can be done in a prompt and timely manner.

Rendimiento de Departamentos de Redes Sociales

Ecuaciones de Números Complejos

Source: https://infune.blogspot.com/ Complex numbers.

In developing a management system with a social network approach, it is necessary to understand that different departments may be involved, such as analytics, content and marketing.In the case of the analytics department, it will collect relevant information on market needs, and once it has obtained an important summary that information can be key to the development of new products within the social network with a management system approach.

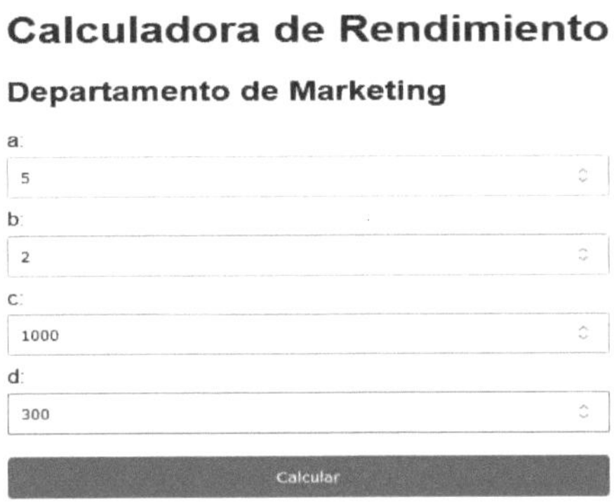

## Calculadora de Rendimiento

### Departamento de Marketing

a:

5

b:

2

c:

1000

d:

300

Calcular

Source: https://infune.blogspot.com/ Marketing department performance.

In the case of the marketing and content department, they must work together, as all those dreams that are coming true for the users must be disseminated through the marketing department.Definitely by referring to the so-called smart indicators, the marketing department can make a successful campaign with the use of AI-supported images that are in the framework of the content that is being developed within the programmes. So it could be assessed for example that a successful social media campaign can drive in a period of one year approximately 100,000 new subscribers, definitely exceeding that target would be something that should really be celebrated within the whole organisation. In this case a programme is made that incorporates the number of successful campaigns in the marketing department, failed campaigns, average campaign reach, and engagement achieved.

**Calculadora de Rendimiento**

**Departamento de Marketing**

a:

| 2 | ⇕ |

b:

| 2 | ⇕ |

c:

| 2 | ⇕ |

d:

| 2 | ⇕ |

Calcular

**Resultado: 0 + 8i**

Source: https://infune.blogspot.com/ Marketing department performance.

In the framework or context of a marketing department, failed campaigns may occur, but they should be overcome as soon as possible. At that moment the content department can help to contribute to improve what is being done, in this specific case when trying to implement the use of complex numbers, irrational numbers and matrices, we try to dynamise the use of mathematics to enhance the activities within organisations and companies, so that this important element such as productivity is boosted to the maximum. In this case, the resolution of a practical exercise focused on the area of marketing resulted in $0 + 8i$, a value that can be really important, especially if we consider i as the positive impression of people and managers to be able to make practical decisions in terms of the management of their companies or organisations. In this way, a positive contribution can be made with the use of mathematics, applying imaginary calculations taking as a reference certain scales that allow the person to quantitatively evaluate the perception of the systems that are being implemented within the social network as a function of effective and proactive management.

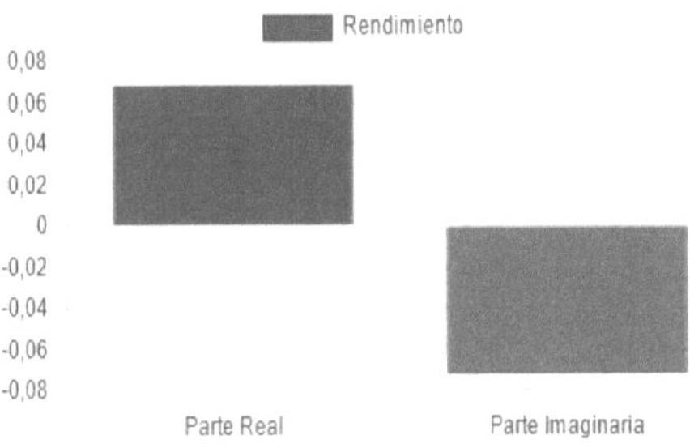


Source: https://infune.blogspot.com/ Performance content department.

When trying to develop a social network focused enterprise from home or if you have grown and integrated departments, it is necessary to be able to have a content department that is efficient, capable of generating topical content so that people feel identified with the social network. It is necessary to understand that in the case of social networks the relationship of content can be linked to creativity, and in the case of generating content that goes viral it can be much more efficient than a hundred others that maintain a traditional behaviour.

**Calculadora de Rendimiento**

**Departamento de Contenido**

e:
10

f:
10

g:
10

h:
10

Calcular

Source: https://infune.blogspot.com/ Performance content department.

Definitely when evaluating the content department, when referring to the amount of interactions that the content gets, yes it is definitely a fundamental element that should be taken into account. To the extent that a new content generates more interactions it should be taken more into account, for example, if a template is created within the social network that allows people to calculate complex numbers and gives good results it can not only be maintained, but a scale should be added to evaluate the results of imaginary content or calculations that may be implicit within an equation. Basically, what we should try to do when we observe an increase in interactions is to find a way to give the user what he/she has been getting in a simplified or extended improved form. In a management system, it is necessary to take into consideration all these quantitative aspects, which lead to providing the manager with these mathematical tools, in order to be able to visualise in time the circumstances of efficiency, effectiveness and productivity that occur in the departments.

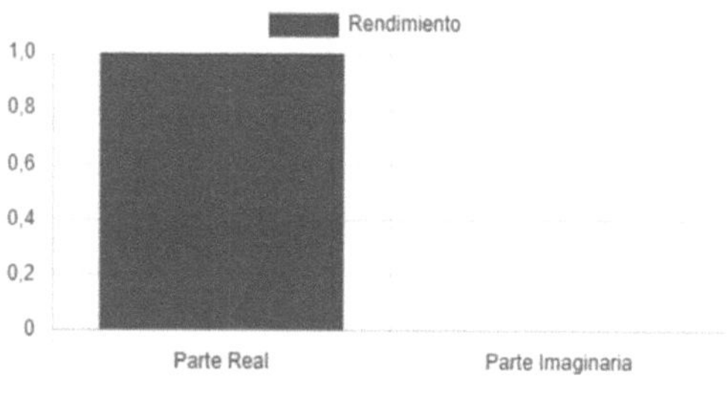


Source: https://infune.blogspot.com/ Performance content department.

In a department of content generation for a social network, it is important to take into consideration the time in which a certain activity is developed, it is necessary to indicate that nowadays, with the emergence of artificial intelligence, what was traditionally done with object programming, today is simply simplified with a voice instruction or with the introduction through the keyboard of a prompt, which represents the possibility that a neural processor, traditional or quantum can interpret an instruction that is related in written form and convert it into an or many images. Regarding the review of the content that is being developed within a department, it is necessary to understand that this can take some time, and definitely to the extent that it takes more hours to review a content, then obviously the total quality of the final result must be guaranteed. However, if we have the capacity to implement new artificial intelligence technologies that allow a higher level of quality in the final result, the time invested in the revision of the final content will surely be reduced proportionally.

## Calculadora de Eficacia

Eficacia HTML:

2

Eficacia JavaScript:

2

Eficacia CSS:

2

Calcular

Source: https://infune.blogspot.com/ Efficiency system.

The effectiveness in this system of complex equations would be oriented towards the development in HTML, Java Script, CSS, in order to evaluate the effectiveness of each of these programmes in the application environment of the management system, it is necessary to understand that CSS would provide the styles of the system, Java Script would allow the development of the formulas and HTML the general configuration of the system. In this case, when solving these values, the result would be 4.24, which would be a qualitative imaginative value that could be associated with the integration of these programming elements into the general system.

# CHAPTER II

## OSCAR ENRIQUE CORREA MIRANDA

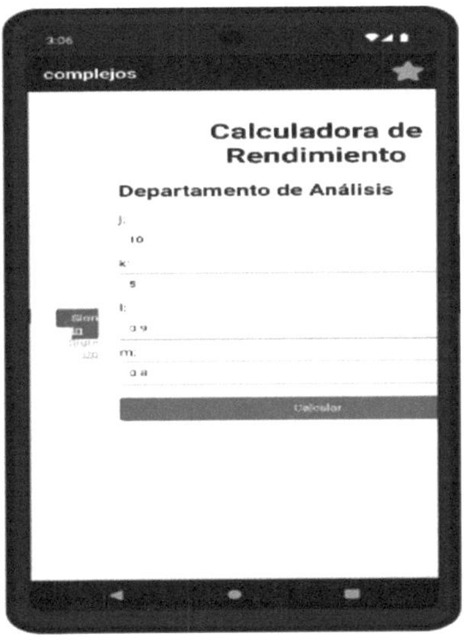

Source: https://infune.blogspot.com/ App performance analysis.

Definitely when you try to implement a mathematical model that integrates complex equations, irrationals and matrices, you are developing an effort that aims to support those managers and business leaders in the proper implementation of their management systems. By taking into consideration the social network analytics department, the existing patterns of relationships between users should be assessed, and reports can be generated that allow all users of the social network to understand their behaviour and interactions with other users and with the social network as such.

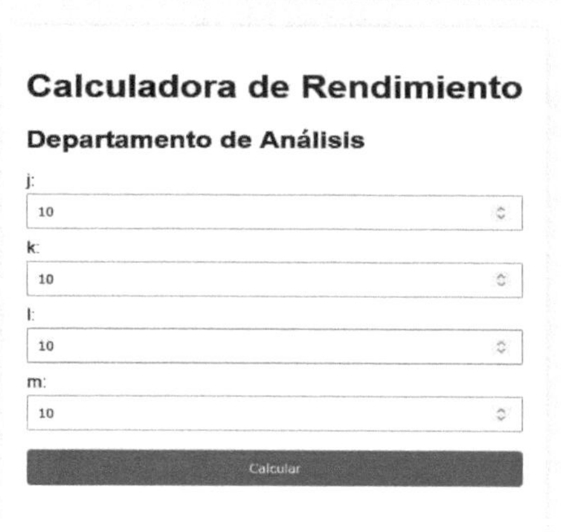



Source: https://infune.blogspot.com/ Performance analysis department.

It is necessary to understand that the analytics department of a social network must keep the metrics associated with the performance of the application, it is therefore necessary to understand that if the marketing department is developing an advertising campaign to promote the artificial intelligence content of the social network applied to mathematics, then it should definitely generate a directly proportional result that has to do with the subscription of people or companies related to the topic that is trying to spread.

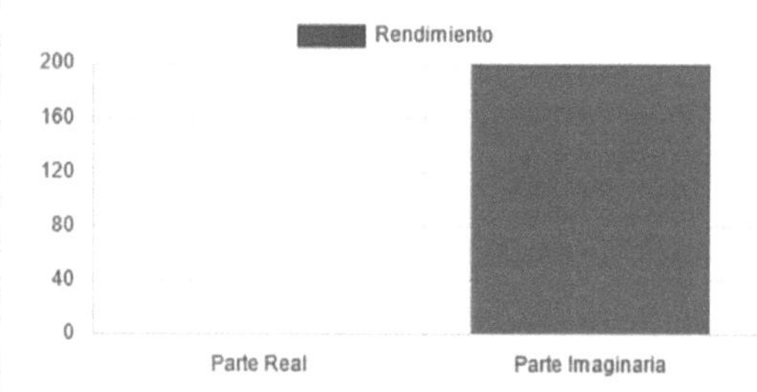



Source: https://infune.blogspot.com/ Performance Chart.

The accuracy of the reports generated by the analysis department is really crucial, in many cases it is required to have influence on the inhabitants of these developed countries, to be able to attract customers who can potentially sponsor the activities that are being developed within the social network.

In this sense, it would be essential to have an analysis of all IP addresses that are accessing the server, in order to determine how many users are accessing from developed or developing countries.

## Calculadora de Rendimiento

### Departamento de Análisis

j:

10

k:

4

l:

3

m:

2

Calcular

Source: https://infune.blogspot.com/ Performance.

In terms of the speed of the department's analysis, it is necessary to understand that often handling this type of statistics in a graphical way can represent the possibility to perform much faster and more in-depth analysis.

It is now necessary to understand that many social networks are trying to focus on the inhabitants of these developed countries, which is in theory where the large companies that can sponsor advertising campaigns that are beneficial to the company's net income are located.It is therefore imperative not only to analyse the IP addresses that are entering the main server, but also to have the possibility of having a programme that transforms these addresses into a graphic that represents the different continents of the planet Earth, and with different shades of colour will in turn show how many people are accessing from each of the countries.

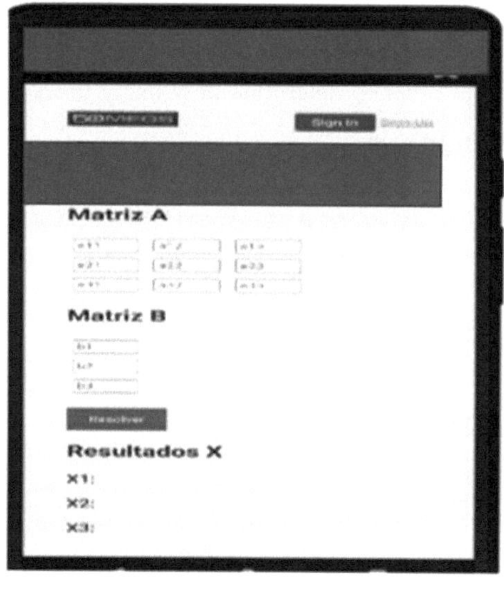

Source: https://infune.blogspot.com/ App equation matrix.

It is necessary to understand matrix equations that focus directly on multivariate computation, in this example two departments of the social network are addressed which can be content and marketing. Theoretically, as positive interactions based on respect, communication and the desire for mutual progress increase, the results of these matrices should be much higher, indicating that interaction leads to higher levels of productivity.

**Resolución de Ecuación Matricial**

**Matriz A**

**Matriz B**

Resolver

**Resultados X**

X1:

X2:

X3:

Source: https://infune.blogspot.com/ Matrix Equation.

It is necessary to understand that in a matrix calculation, not only the relationships between departments can be addressed, but also the performance of the interaction between departments can be represented. Theoretically, the higher the performance values obtained, the better the interactions that have been developed are working.As a practical example, the relationship between the content and marketing department could be expressed, the higher the returns obtained in theory, the more advertising campaigns could be reaching a greater number of users, which is reflected in accurate registrations within the social network.

Source: https://infune.blogspot.com/ Matrix.

With regard to the results observed, the analytics obtained from the entry of different users to the social network will allow us to understand how much the work carried out has managed to increase the reach to the expected audience globally. In this case, as a result of the interactions, the value -1 was obtained, in terms of performance -2 and the final result 5.Definitely, based on this analysis, actions should be promoted between departments to increase the level of interactions that lead to a higher performance, maintaining the results obtained or, in the best case, trying to establish innovative ideas to further increase them.

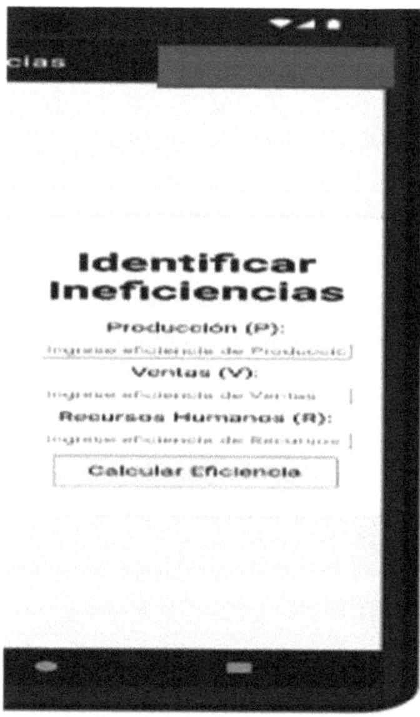


Source: https://infune.blogspot.com/ App inefficiencies.

In the object of study an application is developed to identify inefficiencies in three departments focused on sales production and human resources, in that sense when you are developing a social network business obviously has an internal customer that is represented by the human resource, to the extent that it is trained in new information technologies and artificial intelligence, you could get better results in terms of the final product. It is important to understand that the social network being developed with a focus on integration of mathematical equations and applications, while not initially offering a tangible product directly for sale, does seek to sustain operations through those special revenues that may come from the insertion of advertising from a third party company within the social network.

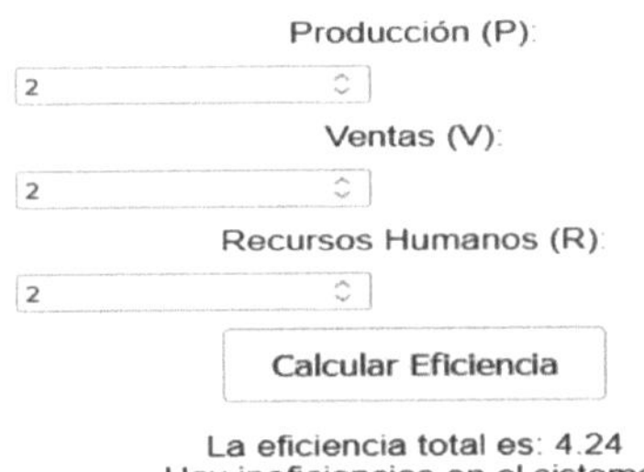



Source: https://infune.blogspot.com/ Efficiency.

As for the production department in the object of study, reference could be made to that area focused on design and programming, on the one hand, as new, more eye-catching and creative designs are developed, this can help people feel more engaged or want to interact more with the system over time. The programming area in this case focuses on developing programmes based on mathematical equations, which lead to solving problems in the different departments of a social network. It is necessary to understand that, in this case, when talking about inefficiencies in the performance of the departments, the lower the losses or errors in the programmes, the lower the inefficiencies will definitely be referred to. In this practical example, the value number 22 is taken into consideration for the departments of production, sales and human resources, and the calculations gave a final efficiency result of 14.07. Definitely when we refer to efficiency we can highlight the relationship that exists when carrying out the desired activities, while a high level of effectiveness can determine that the activities are being carried out in a short period of time, thus maximising the use of the hours. An acceptable level of efficiency refers to the fact that goals can be met progressively, in order to be able to provide a timely response to customers, which in this case are all users who connect through the server on the social network.

# Identificar Ineficiencias



Source: https://infune.blogspot.com/ Efficiency.

Definitely in any social network that is starting up it is required to increase sales to the maximum, so it is essential that the sales department relates directly with the analytics department that manages the metrics focused directly on the impact of the social network in the various countries of the world. In this sense, there are nowadays companies in developed countries that offer telework to many people from home, in some cases they are called online work services companies, in which people can perform different activities such as translations, programming or simply provide customer service via telephone. In this sense, a social network can establish a small advertising space for these types of companies and thus develop a profitable relationship. In the case that a social network is being developed with a focus on mathematical equations supported by programmes and applications, relationships can be established with large social networks by developing multimedia content that explains the benefits of using this social network at the student, managerial or governmental level.

## Identificar Ineficiencias

Producción (P):

333

Ventas (V):

333

Recursos Humanos (R):

333

Calcular Eficiencia

La eficiencia total es: 54.74
El sistema está funcionando de manera óptima.

Source: https://infune.blogspot.com/ Inefficiencies.

In this case, when assigning values to the production, sales and human resources departments equal to 333, the final efficiency obtained was 54.74, which is a substantial improvement with respect to the previously solved exercise. In this case, by solving this irrational equation through this programme, it was possible to determine that as the values associated with production, sales and human resources are increased, the overall efficiency level obtained in the social network can also be increased proportionally.This type of calculation allows us to understand that the production department is generating new content that captures the attention of users, when the staff is being trained in a better way around new technologies to implement programmes that are effective, eye-catching, and in addition to this, it is possible to establish relationships with third party companies that contribute positively to the performance of the social network. In that instant, a higher level of efficiency will be achieved globally in the social network, which in the beginning could be represented in a higher level of user satisfaction.The number of new entrants to the network or simply a substantial increase in the level of registration of established users in the network in the short term of one year.



Source: https://infune.blogspot.com/ Effectiveness.

In this case, an efficiency calculator is incorporated into the management system, which will allow measuring the activities carried out in HTML, Java Script, CSS, in this case, assigning a value of 2 to each element, a final result of 4.24 efficiency was obtained.

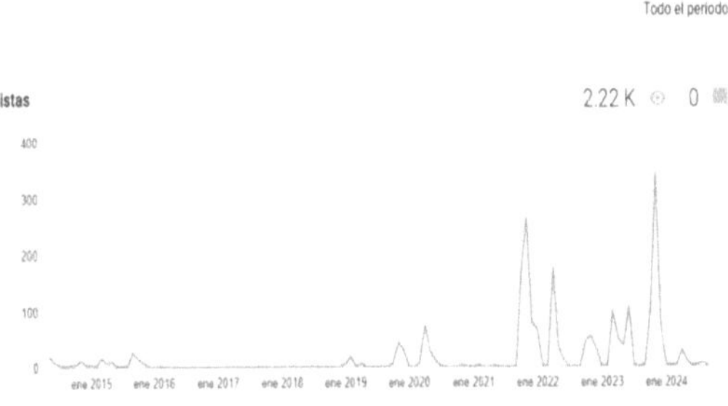


Source: https://infune.blogspot.com/ Vistas.

When teaching management information systems, it is necessary to try to incorporate as many interacting systems as possible, as participants are hungry for system knowledge that will enable them to manage the institutions or organisations they are interested in managing or are already managing.In this case they were assigned a blog, so that they could study each of the units established within the management vision of the systems they intend to teach, developing videos and multimedia images in order to try to impact the five senses of the students accessing the information. The contact via WhatsApp not only allows the presentation of the attendance lists where the students and the teacher are listed, but also the possibility to structurally present during each week of the course of study those assignments that are due The participants will develop their skills under the supervision of the lecturer.

Source: https://infune.blogspot.com/ URL.

In this case it can be said that confidence is earned, which means that to the extent that the participants observe that the content is up to date, incorporates mathematical and computer tools for possible use in the labour market, this gives the student the security required to feel that the time they are spending studying the management information systems curriculum unit will, in the end, be totally valid because it will contribute positively to their effective professional training.

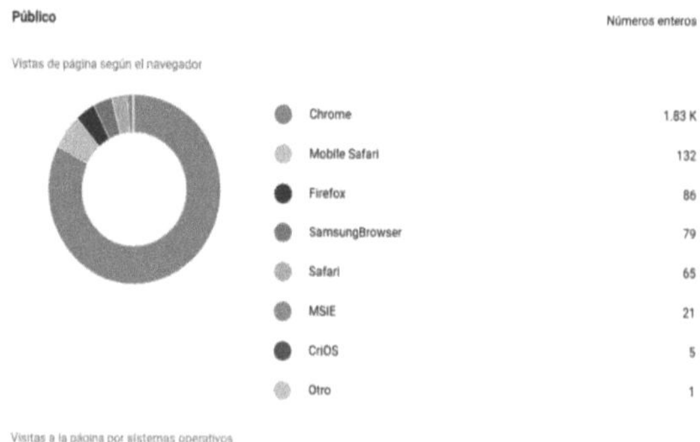



Source: https://infune.blogspot.com/ Operating systems.

In summary, developing computer systems that take into consideration equations of complex numbers, irrational numbers and linear matrices is an extremely gratifying project both for students of the curricular unit of management information systems and for company leaders who require tangible tools to be able to manage their organisations in an effective way, taking into consideration quantitative elements that allow them to positively transform the reality that they observe in the different departments that they have to manage.In short, in this research it is possible to determine that it is possible to take into consideration intelligent indicators, which, when related and evaluated from the perspective of equations of irrational imaginary numbers and matrices, allow directors and managers of institutions to manage their organisations in a much more effective way today. The challenge of developing a management system from the perspective of a social network is a truly significant commitment that in this research is achieved through the development of a local server with the progressive incorporation of Java Script, HTML, CSS and PHP technology.

# BIBLIOGRAPHICAL REFERENCES

IIPE UNESCO (2021). Uses of information systems in educational policy planning and management in Latin America. UNESCO

UNESCO (2021). Modernizing education management through EMIS: strengthening the system after the COVID-19 pandemic. UNESCO

Massón Cruz, R. M., & Torres Saavedra, A. R. (2009). Unesco, policies and education systems in the countries of the Latin American region. VARONA, (48-49)4

UNESCO (2021). Characterization of educational information systems in Latin America. UNESCO

# I want morebooks!

Buy your books fast and straightforward online - at one of world's fastest growing online book stores! Environmentally sound due to Print-on-Demand technologies.

Buy your books online at
## www.morebooks.shop

Kaufen Sie Ihre Bücher schnell und unkompliziert online – auf einer der am schnellsten wachsenden Buchhandelsplattformen weltweit! Dank Print-On-Demand umwelt- und ressourcenschonend produzi ert.

Bücher schneller online kaufen
## www.morebooks.shop